THANKSGIVING

Written by Alice K. Flanagan

Illustrated by Kathie Kelleher

Content Adviser: Professor Sherry L. Field, Department of Social Science Education, College of Education, The University of Georgia

Reading Adviser: Dr. Linda D. Labbo, Department of Reading Education, College of Education, The University of Georgia

COMPASS POINT BOOKS

MINNEAPOLIS, MINNESOTA

Compass Point Books
3722 West 50th Street, #115
Minneapolis, MN 55410

Visit Compass Point Books on the Internet at *www.compasspointbooks.com*
or e-mail your request to *custserv@compasspointbooks.com*

Editors: E. Russell Primm and Emily J. Dolbear
Designer: The Design Lab

Library of Congress Cataloging-in-Publication Data

Flanagan, Alice K.
     Thanksgiving / written by Alice K. Flanagan ; illustrated by Kathie Kelleher.
     p. cm. — (Holidays and festivals)
   Includes bibliographical references and index.
   ISBN 0-7565-0087-7 (hardcover : lib bdg.)
     1. Thanksgiving Day—Juvenile literature. [1. Thanksgiving Day. 2. Holidays.]
I. Kelleher, Kathie, ill. II. Title. III. Series.
   GT4975 .F59 2002
   394.2649—dc21   2001001507

Table of Contents

A turkey, a football game,
and maybe a parade —you can see
all of these things on Thanksgiving Day.

Thanksgiving Day is an American holiday. People in the United States **celebrate** Thanksgiving on the fourth Thursday of November.

On this day, most families gather to share a meal. They give thanks for the good things in their lives. Some people also watch football games and parades.

Giving Thanks for a Good Harvest

It's true that the first Thanksgiving took place in America in 1621. Giving thanks for food began long before that, however.

For centuries, people all over the world have been giving thanks at **harvest time**. After farmers gathered in their crops, they often held a feast.

At this feast, they ate the food from their harvest. Then they danced and played games. Sometimes they even held parades. Today, around the world, people celebrate Thanksgiving in the same way.

Harvest Festivals
Around the World

Long ago, in China, the moon was part of the harvest celebration. The Chinese called their three-day **festival** *Chung Ch'ui*. They thought the moon looked brighter and rounder at that time of year. They said it was the moon's birthday.

Women made tasty moon cakes from the harvest grain. Then they held a big feast. Children played games. Everyone gave thanks for the wonderful food. At night, men played music in the moonlight.

The Romans called their harvest festival Cerelia. This festival honored the corn goddess Ceres. The word cereal comes from her name.

People began the celebration with a long parade through the fields. Then they shared a big feast. They danced and played music. Some people played games.

People who lived in North and South America had harvest festivals, too. Corn was their most important crop. They also grew potatoes, squash, beans, and peanuts.

The Aztec and Maya peoples were the first to grow corn in large fields. At festival time, the Aztec and Maya had fun. They played games and held contests. They ate well too. The Maya ate turkey at their feast.

In Europe, each country had its own way of celebrating the harvest. In England, the festival was called harvest home. In Scotland, it was known as the Kern.

Why the Pilgrims Came to America

Long ago, the people of England were unhappy with their church leaders. Some of them decided to go to America to start their own church. These people were called **Pilgrims**.

The Pilgrims sailed to America on a ship called the *Mayflower*. On December 26, 1620, the ship landed in what is now the state of Massachusetts. The Pilgrims called their new home Plymouth. That was the name of the town they had left behind in England.

It was winter in Plymouth. The Pilgrims needed food right away. They had to build houses. Many Pilgrims got sick. More than half of them died.

The Pilgrims and Indians Help One Another

In the spring, the Pilgrims made friends with an Indian. His name was Squanto. He was from the Wampanoag tribe.

Squanto set up a meeting between the Pilgrims and the Wampanoag. The Pilgrims and the Indians signed a paper. This paper said they would live in peace and help one another. This kind of agreement is called a **treaty**. The treaty lasted for fifty years.

Squanto lived with the Pilgrims. He taught them about plants and animals. He showed them how to search for eels. Squanto also taught the Pilgrims how to make sugar. He helped them plant corn, beans, and squash together. Without Squanto's help, many more Pilgrims would have died.

In the fall, the Pilgrims and the Wampanoag held a feast. They thanked God for the good harvest. The Pilgrims and Indians ate fish, wild turkey, geese, ducks, and deer. They made breads, puddings, and even popcorn!

The Pilgrims and Indians learned from one another. They learned different ways of cooking and eating food. They shared different ways of praying, hunting, and playing games.

Some people think that the harvest festival in 1620 was the first American Thanksgiving. But harvest feasts were not new to Native Americans. Long before the English came to America, the Wampanoag had thanksgiving feasts.

The English had thanksgiving feasts before 1620, too. In 1607, the English celebrated a harvest feast in Maine. In 1619, the new arrivals gave thanks for a safe landing in Virginia.

A New Nation Gives Thanks

The people who moved from England to America were called **colonists**. The communities they built were called **colonies**. The colonists often held thanksgiving feasts. They gave thanks for good fortune, such as weddings. They also celebrated good weather or a big harvest.

By 1770, there were thirteen British colonies in America. In 1775, they went to war with Britain to be free. In 1776, the Declaration of Independence was signed and the United States was born. The Revolutionary War lasted until 1783 when the colonists won. Every time the colonists won a battle, they gave thanks.

George Washington became the first president. He named November 26, 1789, a day of national thanksgiving. Americans prayed and feasted. For many years, however, America had no official Thanksgiving Day.

A Special Day of Thanksgiving

The idea of an official Thanksgiving started with a writer named Sarah Hale. She suggested that people in the United States celebrate Thanksgiving on the same day.

Many people read about her idea. They started celebrating Thanksgiving on November 26. People who moved west brought the practice with them. By the 1850s, many states celebrated Thanksgiving on the same day.

Thanksgiving was an important family event. Everyone helped prepare for it. Women made pies and cakes. Men hunted animals and dug up vegetables. Even children helped out around the farm.

Sharing was a big part of Thanksgiving. People brought baskets of food to their schoolteachers. Bosses gave gifts to their workers. Neighbors shared with neighbors. People brought meals to the needy.

A National Holiday

In 1861, the United States had a civil war. Some states in the South broke away from the states in the North. The Southern states set up their own government. They called themselves the Confederate States of America.

President Abraham Lincoln believed the states should stay together. The president asked men in the North to fight for the country. The war lasted four years. The North won. The Southern states rejoined the Northern states.

During the war, President Abraham Lincoln called for a day of thanksgiving. On November 26, 1863, the president announced that the last Thursday in November would be Thanksgiving Day.

Then, in 1941, Thanksgiving Day became a national holiday celebrated on the fourth Thursday of November. It was a holiday for all Americans.

A THANKSGIVING DAY PROCLAMATION

Thanksgiving is a holiday in Canada too. It is celebrated on the second Monday of October.

Today, businesses and offices are closed on Thanksgiving. Most people have the day off from work.

Things You Might See on Thanksgiving Day

Parades

Parades have long been a part of the Thanksgiving celebration. In the past, farmers put on parades during harvest time. They packed their wagons full of crops. They decorated them with flowers. Then they pulled the colorful wagons through the villages.

Today, we have **floats** with storybook characters and movie stars riding on them. Huge balloons fly above the floats. We have music and marching bands.

Can you name the big parades? Macy's department store parade is in New York City. The city of Philadelphia has a Thanksgiving Day parade. There is a parade in Hollywood, California, too.

The Pilgrims

The Pilgrims who landed in America in 1620 wore very plain clothing. They had strong religious beliefs. They read the Bible every day and went to church.

Everyone in a Pilgrim family worked hard. Parents were firm with their children. Each child in a Pilgrim family had a job to do. A young boy might gather nuts or berries. A young girl might help at home by rocking a baby's cradle.

The Wampanoag

The Pilgrims called Native Americans "Indians." The Native Americans in that area called themselves *Wampanoag*. They farmed and fished there long before the Pilgrims came.

The Wampanoag showed the Pilgrims how to survive in America. After many years, the Pilgrims took over the Wampanoag's land.

Today, many Wampanoag refuse to take part in the Thanksgiving holiday. It reminds them of the time when their land was stolen from them.

The Mayflower

The Pilgrims sailed to America on a ship called the *Mayflower*. The voyage was dangerous, long, and tiring. It took more than two months.

The ship was very crowded. There were one hundred adults and thirty-three children on the *Mayflower*.

Most people slept on the deck in all kinds of weather. It was often cold and rainy. There were many storms.

People ate cold food. They had very little fresh water. Once the food and water on the ship was gone, there would be no more. It was hard for people to keep clean. Many people got sick during the trip. Two people died.

Turkey, Cranberries, and Pumpkin Pie

At most Thanksgiving dinners today, people eat turkey, cranberries, and pumpkin pie. Many people believe that the Pilgrims and the Wampanoag enjoyed these foods at their harvest feast. At that time, wild turkeys roamed the woods and cranberries grew wild. The Wampanoag used cranberries and pumpkins in many of their dishes.

What You Can Do on Thanksgiving Day

Thanksgiving has always been an enjoyable day for family and friends. It is a time to give thanks for the good things in our lives.

We can show our thanks in many ways. Here are some ideas:

* Help make a dish or a pie for dinner.
* Invite a friend to your Thanksgiving celebration.
* Thank the people who take care of you.
* Share what you have with others. Make up a basket of food and bring it to someone who is hungry or lonely.
* If your school or place of worship is collecting food or money for the poor, give what you can.

Glossary

celebrate to have a party or honor a special event

colonies the communities that colonists built in America

colonists the English people who came to America to start new lives

festival a holiday or celebration

floats a decorated truck or platform in a parade

harvest time the time when farmers gather their crops

Pilgrims a group of people from England who moved to America to start their
own church in 1620

treaty an agreement between two governments

Where You Can Learn More about Thanksgiving

At the Library

Anderson, Joan. *The First Thanksgiving Feast.* New York: Clarion Books, 1984.

Berg, Elizabeth. *Festivals of the World: USA.* Milwaukee, Wis.: Gareth Stevens Publishing, 1999.

Hintz, Martin, and Kate Hintz. *Thanksgiving: Why We Celebrate It the Way We Do.* Mankato, Minn.: Capstone Press, 1996.

Penner, Lucille Recht. *The Thanksgiving Book.* New York: Hastings House Publishers, 1986.

On the Web

ONLINE THANKSGIVING RESOURCES AT THE LIBRARY: *http://www.gbalc.org/thanksgiving.htm* For links that relate to Thanksgiving history, songs, crafts, and food

THANKSGIVING ON THE NET: *http://www.holidays.net/thanksgiving/*
For information about Thanksgiving crafts, decorations, and recipes

THE WORLDWIDE HOLIDAY AND FESTIVAL SITE: *http://www.holidayfestival.com/*
For information about holidays and festivals around the world

Index

About the Author and Illustrator

Alice K. Flanagan writes books for children and teachers. Since she was a young girl, she has enjoyed writing. She has written more than seventy books. Some of her books include biographies of U.S. presidents and their wives, biographies of people working in our neighborhoods, phonics books for beginning readers, and informational books about birds and Native Americans. Alice K. Flanagan lives in Chicago, Illinois.

Kathie Kelleher has been an illustrator for more than twenty years. It has been a passion since childhood and she feels fortunate to have made it her career. Some of her work includes the Everything series of books and *Stuck on Presidents*. Kathie Kelleher lives in Massachusetts with her husband, two daughters, and Shelbie, their cat. They live near Plymouth, where the first Thanksgiving took place.